home
on the
range

another incredible cookbook
by nun other than
sister karol jackowski

Ave Maria Press
Notre Dame, Indiana 46556

Rounds of applause for these persons: My very best friends Gloria, wanda, valentina and sister; Hank and shirl the proud parents of us all; the siblings jackie, deb, Hank and david; joan Bellina my editor; coll cannon; Michael dongarra; Michelle Harmon; Lin "Gretka" Heidinger; the almost famous julie jensen; the incredible cook nue nugent; peeve; "Little Miss Debbie" Anne Reid plus jo and ed; Martha Rabaut; kathleen Rice; adri trigiani; Mary seremet; Barb and lin saunders; elmo, eloise and leah; the ali yella family and phyllis zidalis.

A powerful everlasting debt of gratitude to them, to the island of manhattan, to the village i lived in and to the sisters of the Holy Cross who put me there. Stars on us all.

COVER DESIGN: An abstract of nuns at Home on the Range.

TABLE OF CONTENTS

the
simplest
and
most
effective
way
to
sanctity
is to
disappear
into the
BACKGROUND
of
ORDINARY
everyday
Routine.

t. MERTON

♫ This is dedicated... to the ♫ ♫
ones i-i lo-o-o-ve... ♫
to Brian, who like me, will
spend the rest of his life trying
to behave;
to Katie who got her ears pierced
for her first confession;
to jon who thinks i have
Bette Davis eyes and look like
Daisy Duke;
to fairy Godchild ellen who i
held as she got sprung from
Limbo (not a very pretty place for babies);
and to surprise child,
Karalyn or Stanley,
who will soon join
the cast of
wonder tots.
This one's for you.

Splendid and Superior Spinach

you need:
2 10-oz. pks. fresh spinach
6 (that's 🖐️ 👌) hard boiled eggs
1 medium can bean sprouts (drained)
8 slices crisp bacon (crumbled) ↓

〜〜〜 〜〜〜 〜〜〜 〜〜〜 〜〜〜 〜〜〜 〜〜〜

Mix all of that together.
NOW...

When ready to serve you add
this splendid and superior dressing:

½ c. vinegar   ¾ c. brown sugar
⅓ c. chili sauce   1 med. onion (diced)
1 c. salad oil   1 Tbsp. Worcestershire

Blend in blender.
Pour over spinach mixture
thus making the entire
event both splendid and
superior.

STARS ON THIS FRUIT SALAD

TAKE SOME FRUIT LIKE THIS:

GRANNY SMITH OR SOME OTHER
RATHER CRISP TART APPLES
PINEAPPLE
BLUEBERRIES
STRAWBERRIES
PEACHES
PEARS
BANANAS
CANTALOUPE

FIGURE ON A SMALL BITE AND CUT
FRUIT INTO BITE-SIZE PIECES.

THEN GET SOME:
VANILLA YOGURT (HOWEVER MUCH
YOU NEED FOR THE AMOUNT OF
FRUIT YOU HAVE)
FRESH MINT LEAVES CHOPPED UP

MIX IT ALL TOGETHER AND
SERVE AS SALAD, DESSERT
OR SNACK. REAL CLEAN AND
HEALTHY.

BEULAH, PEEL ME A GRAPE. ~MAE WEST

8.

Q-CUMBERS DRESSED in SOUR CREAM

1 nice medium-size Q-cumber
1 tsp. salt
½ c. sour cream
1 Tbsp. vinegar
1 tsp. sugar
1 tsp. dill seed
dash pepper

Cut Q-cumber into very skinny, slim, thin, slender slices and sprinkle with salt. Let those stand around in the salt for 30 minutes or so, then drain thoroughly. Combine sour cream, vinegar, sugar, dill seed and the outstanding dash of pepper. Stir and pour over the very skinny, slim, thin, slender slices now sprinkled with salt. Chill in fridge about 30 min. Serves 4-6 or so.

9.

THE OFTEN INTIMIDATING ARTICHOKE

Rinse artichokes in plain (as opposed to unplain, i guess) water. Trim the stems a little at the bottom and pull off those small bottom leaves. They didn't make it. Then take a scissors and cut off the sharp pointy things on the leaves because they pinch. Take a knife and cut about 1" of leaves from the top. If you have a steamer put artichokes in the steamer with about 3" of water. Add 1 tsp. salt and 1 tsp. lemon juice. If you don't have a steamer you should be ashamed of yourself. If you have no shame but do have friends ask them to buy you one. Cover and boil 30-45 minutes.... or until the base can be pierced easily with a fork. When done remove, peel leaves and dip in →

LEMON BUTTER

1 stick butter slowly melted

½ lemon squeezed into melted
    butter (take seeds out. tacky.)

Dip leaves in butter. Go M-M-M-M.
    makes enough for artichokes.

VINAIGRETTE FOR ARTICHOKES

2 TBsp. wine vinegar
5 TBsp. olive oil
1 TBsp. sour cream
1 TBsp. chopped parsley
1 tsp. seasoned salt
dash garlic powder
dash mustard powder

Mix real well. Dip leaves in that
tasty number. enough for four.

Go buy a jar.

♭ HOW ♪ ARE ♪ THINGS ♪ IN ♪♪ GUACAMOLE...♪

☞ (i.e. 4) LARGE ripe avocados (should be
    soft when you squeeze them)
1/4 c. onion minced
2 LARGE GARLIC cloves
1 small tomato chopped up
1/2 c. chopped GREEN CHILIS (can use the ones
        in the can or jar)
1/8 tsp. GRound cumin
pinch of salt and pepper and GRound
    Red chili powder
1 tBsp. Lemon juice

Peel, take the pit out and coarsely
 mash the avocados. Add the minced
onion. Put GaRlic throUGh a GaRlic
PRess and add to avocados along with
tomato and Green chilis. Add seasonings
and Lemon juice and mix everything
Real well. Chill. Makes enoUGh for 4
(uatro). Serve with Lettuce Leaves and
make it look Real nice. Use taco chips
and dip. BUeno. Bueno. Bueno.

Set your salad off with these

Poppy seed dressing

- 1½ c. sugar
- 2 tsp. dry mustard
- 2 tsp. salt
- ⅔ c. vinegar
- 2 c. salad oil
- 2 tsp. onion juice
- 1 tbsp. poppy seeds

Combine sugar, dry mustard, salt, vinegar and beat together. Add onion juice and beat again. Add salad oil slowly and when it gets thick add seeds. Chill.

GIN YES GIN DRESSING

- 1 c. catsup
- 2 c. sugar
- 1 tsp. worcestershire
- 1 c vinegar
- 1 tsp. salt
- 2 c. oil
- dash tabasco
- 1 med. onion grated
- ¼ c. gin yes gin

Blend in blender. Pour over salad. This is a salad dressing not a drink.

A NICE VINAIGRETTE

½ c. olive oil
¼ c. tarragon vinegar
1 tsp. sugar
½ tsp. salt
½ tsp. dijon mustard

¼ tsp. paprika
1 tsp. of your
favorite herb
(basil, chives, etc.)
2 garlic cloves

Put all of that in a jar. Cover and
shake well. Let it stand overnight.
Remove garlic cloves before serving.

*CELERY SEED

← celery seeds

½ c. sugar
1 tsp. dry mustard
1 tsp. salt
1-2 tsp. celery seed
Combine those, then add:
   1 tbsp. grated onion
Gradually add:
   1 c. salad oil
   ⅓ c. vinegar
   Blend well.
* Best made in a blender because
you see ☞ ☜ constant beating is a must.

THE BEST VEGETABLE DIP IN THE WORLD

1 cup mayonnaise
1 cup sour cream
1/4 cup water chestnuts chopped up
1/8 tsp. garlic powder
1/8 tsp. salt
1/4 cup parsley
1/4 cup chopped onion

Mix. Serve. Say thank you very much when everyone says how good this is. Do not give them the recipe. Tell them where to buy this book.

✻ A TRULY FASCINATING FACT ✻

COOKBOOKS OUTSELL SEX BOOKS IN THE UNITED STATES.

HIT THE SAUCE

THE ABOVE FIGURES ILLUSTRATE
THE LOOKS OF A WHOLE FLOCK
OF SHEEP WHO HAVE HIT THE SAUCE.

16.

YOUR BASIC WHITE SAUCE

2 tBsp. Butter
2 tBsp. flour
1 cup Heated Milk*
Basic seasonings, salt, white pepper

Melt Butter in a skillet and sprinkle flour in. Cook it a few minutes kind of mixing it around with a fork. While that's going on Heat the milk to Scalding. When the flour is pretty well mixed remove the pan and wait for it to stop BUBBLING. Then pour the milk in and stir real fast. When it's all well mixed then put it Back on the heat and let it simmer for several minutes. Stir often. Season with salt and pepper. Think about tossing these Hot numbers in for some PIZZAZZ. → → → → → → →

* SOUR MILK MAKES for a tasty
flavor and that's the truth.

PIZZAZZ

YOUR BASIC WHITE SAUCE ADDITIONS:

HERBS: ¼ tsp. of your favorite. Like BASIL, thyme, parsley, tarragon or whatever. Add two if so moved.

WINE: Couple of tablespoons of dry white wine or white vermouth.

ZIP: 1 tsp. or so: Lemon juice, lime juice, worcestershire sauce (Good for fish).

VEGGIES: Dice, sauté and add carrots, onion, MUSHROOMS, Green pepper.

CHEESE: Grate your favorite cheese and add to taste.

- OR -

- the pièce de résistance -

Sliced toasted almonds
in the sauce or
SPRINKLED on top.

18.   ZOW.

CHEESE  SAUCE

Do the Basic white sauce.
When it's nice and smooth and hot,
Reduce Heat and add 1 c. Grated
Cheese of whatever kind. Season
with: ½ tsp. salt
        sprinkles of paprika
        parsley
        cayenne pepper sprinkled
        dry mustard sprinkles

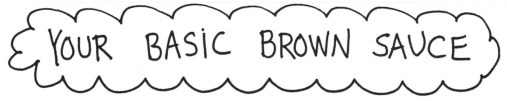

YOUR BASIC BROWN SAUCE

Ready now? Remember that
tasty white sauce? Well with this one
you follow the same procedure except
you cook the flour and butter until
flour is well browned. Use:
    2 tbsp. Butter
    2 tbsp. flour
    1 c. Heated Liquid Like water
      or vegetable stock (⅓ c.
      of vermouth is nice)

★ White wine Sauce ★

Heat 2 tBsp. Butter and sauté 2
tBsp. Chopped onion. Stir in
1½ tBsp. flour. Stir in little
By little :
　　　　½ c. Chicken Bouillon
　　　　½ c. dry white wine
Add 1 tBsp. parsley or Chives or
almonds. Salt as needed.
Absolutely elegant.

HERB BUTTER

Melt: 2-3 tBsp. Butter*
Blend in : 1 tsp. fresh lemon
　　　　　　　　　　juice
　　　　　　¼ tsp. Herb salt
Add: 2-3 tBsp. of your
　　favorite HERB
　　　　OR
　　1 clove Garlic minced
Blend. Serve over veggies,
　　　fish, whatever.

* 1 tBsp. per serving.

COCKTAIL SAUCE

1½ c. catsup
1 tbsp. Lemon juice
1 tbsp. Worcestershire
2 tbsp. Horseradish
1½ tsp. Sugar
Big dash Hot pepper sauce
Salt and pepper
Combine and chill.

MAKE YOUR OWN HERB SALT...

2 tbsp. salt
2 tsp. each... Oregano and sweet Basil
1 tsp. thyme
1 tsp. onion powder
½ tsp. Garlic powder
½ tsp. paprika

Mix. Sprinkle here, there and everywhere.

21.

THE always economical still RELIABLE and EVER ELEGANT CHICKEN

→
→
→

↑
THIS is a CHICKEN disguised as a sheep in a BRilliant attempt to avoid an untimely death.

↑
OBVIOUSLY HAPPY WITH NEW-FOUND IDENTITY.

↑
another BRIGHt one.

22.

★ The Amazing Jen-sen Chicken ★

Preheat oven to 325°.
Get out a 12" black cast iron skillet.
Buy a whole chicken weighing in at
3 LBS. Wash it, take the insides out
and put them on the side. Put the
chicken in the pan. Take paprika and
sprinkle the chicken all over until it
looks bright pink. Then take garlic
powder and sprinkle the chicken again.
Don't be afraid to sprinkle too much.
Then take salt and pepper and sprinkle
that all over. Don't miss any spots.
Put the now well sprinkled chicken
chest up in the frying pan. Put
the gizzard, livers, etc. next to it
and sprinkle those with the same
seasonings. Cover loosely with
foil and bake in oven for 2 HRS.
Take the foil off for the last 20 min.
so the chicken gets crisp. And there
you have it: the Amazing Jen-sen
chicken.

For Gizzard Lovers Only

1 LB. CHICKEN GIZZARDS
2 CLOVES GARLIC
1 LARGE onion CHOPPED
1 TBSP. CHOPPED PARSLEY
1/4 c. VEGETABLE OIL
1/2 tsp. SALT
1/4 tsp. PEPPER
1/2 c. WATER
1/4 c. VEGETABLE OIL
1/3 c. WINE VINEGAR

COOK PRECIOUS GIZZARDS in pot of water (enough to cover) for 1 or 1½ HRS. COVER pot half way. DRAIN and COOL. WHILE that's GOING on peel GARLIC, CHOPPED onions and PARSLEY. WHEN GIZZARDS are COOL SLICE them UP. In a LARGE skillet heat 1/4c. OIL. Add onions, PARSLEY, GARLIC, Salt and pepper. STIR, COVER and simmer for 10 min. Add GIZZARDS and STIR. Add water. Then REST of OIL. Then VINEGAR. COVER and simmer 10 min. MORE. SERVE OVER noodles, RICE, MASHED potatoes, the kitchen sink OR WHATEVER.

FOR GIZZARD LOVERS ONLY

Marinate ½ LB. Chicken Livers in
Marsala wine (just enough to cover)
for 1 HOUR. In a skillet sauté:

- 4 tBsp. Butter
- ¼ c. scallions
- ½ c. mushrooms chopped (fresh)

Pat Livers dry and sprinkle Lightly
with flour. Add to onions and
mushrooms and sauté 3-4 min.
Stir in:
- 1 tBsp. fresh Lemon juice
- ⅓ c. Marsala wine
- ½ tsp. sweet Basil
- ¼ tsp. salt
- ⅛ tsp. pepper

Cook over medium Heat 6-8 min.
Stir every now and then. Serve
with Rice.

for Liver Lovers only

KNOCK YOUR SOCKS OFF CHICKEN

3 LBS. of your favorite parts of chicken. Sprinkle with salt and pepper. Marinate 2-3 hours in 1 cup dry white wine. Cover.

Remove chicken. Save marinade. Sauté pieces in 2 tbsp. of butter until golden brown. Remove chicken and set aside. Add 1 onion finely chopped and 1 minced garlic clove to skillet. Sauté 2 min. Then sprinkle with 1 tsp. flour. Cook & stir for 2 more min. Add reserved marinade.

Then... back to the chicken.

Put chicken back in the skillet and add:

    ½ tsp. salt.
    ⅛ tsp. pepper
    ⅛ tsp. paprika
    ½ tsp. basil
    3 tsp. chopped fresh parsley →

Cover and simmer 30-35 min.
Then once again remove chicken
and add to skillet:

   1 LB. fresh sliced mushrooms

Mix and add:

   ¼ c. Half and Half
   1 egg yolk Beaten
   2-3 tBsp. sauce from skillet

Cook and stir to thicken sauce.
Adjust seasonings to taste. Pour
over chicken. Serve. Get your
socks knocked off. Honest to God.
no lie.

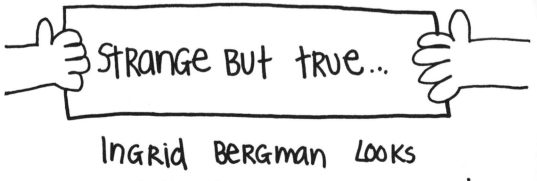

STRANGE BUT TRUE...

   Ingrid Bergman looks
      just like Karol Jackowski.

☆ *ROCKY 4 ☆

6-8 of your favorite pieces of chicken
8 tBsp. flour divided into 4+4
1 tsp. salt
¼ tsp. pepper
2 tBsp. Butter
2 tBsp. cooking oil
½ c diced onion
½ tsp. tarragon
1 10-oz. can chicken Broth
1 c. apple cider
½ lemon squeezed
½ c. heavy cream

Mix 4 tBsp. flour, salt and pepper in
a plastic Bag. Add chicken and shake
your Booty and the Bag until the chicken
looks pretty well coated. Put Butter
and oil in skillet and heat. Add
chicken and cook till Brown. Add rest
of flour, onion and tarragon, sautéing
chicken 5 min. or so making sure
it's well coated................⌐

*The chicken that won once and for all.

28.

MORE ROCKY 4

Now, as i was saying, the next thing you do is take a sauce pan and heat the CHICKEN BROTH, CIDER and LEMON juice. Add to CHICKEN in FRYING pan. COVER and SIMMER aBout ½ hour. then REMOVE CHICKEN. Add CREAM to sauce in skillet, stiRRiNG constantly. When well MIXEd POUR OVER CHICKEN and SERVE.

♩ Na-Na-Na- Naaaah ♫
Na-Na- Na -Naaaah ...

Moments to Live By

The BIBLE says that CHRISTIANS SHOULd KISS one another.

Romans
16:16

HOT CHICKEN SALAD

4 c. chopped cooked chicken
1½ c. diced celery
½ c. chopped toasted almonds
1 can (small) water chestnuts, sliced
3 Tbsp. minced onion
1½ Tbsp. lemon juice
pepper to taste
1 c. mayonnaise

Mix together. Cover with:
    1½ c. grated cheddar cheese
    1½ c. crushed potato chips
Bake at 375° for 25 min.

GET THIS

snakes have no eyelids.

Beef-Chicken Marinade for
★★★ MILLIONS ★★★

1½ c. soy sauce
6 c. pineapple juice
½ c. sugar
½ c. cider vinegar
1 tsp. garlic powder
2 c. sherry
1½ tsp. salt

Mix liquid. Mix dry stuff. Mix together. Marinate 24 hours before cooking. Dynamite for Barbeque. Makes a lot. You can freeze some. It's eternal and everlasting.

THIS IS TRUE

Grape juice will quench your thirst better than beer.

The Best Barbecue Ribs Ever

4 LBS. SPARERIBS OR COUNTRY STYLE RIBS CUT INTO SERVING size pieces

1 C. BROWN SUGAR (Round firm and fully packed)

½ C. CHILI SAUCE

¼ C. CATSUP

¼ C. DARK RUM

¼ C. SOY SAUCE

¼ C. WORCESTERSHIRE

1 tsp. DRY MUSTARD

2 CLOVES GARLIC (CRUSHED)

dash of pepper

WRAP RIBS in double thickness of foil and BAKE FOR 1½ HR. at 350°. Unwrap and drain drippings. Combine ingredients and pour over RIBS. MARINATE at ROOM temperature FOR 1 HR. OR in fridge FOR 2 HRS. When Ready, Bake at 350° FOR 30 min. MORE BASTING with sauce. OR GRILL FOR 30 min. MORE ABOUT 4" above coals turning and Basting with sauce. Makes 3-4. THERE is no doubt that this is the very Best.

● *B.S. PORK CHOPS ●

4 center-cut chops about 1" thick
3 tbsp. butter
1 green onion
½ c. seasoned bread crumbs
1 tbsp. chopped fresh parsley
¼ tsp. salt
dash pepper
¼ tsp. rosemary

Stuffing: Melt butter and remove from heat. Chop green onion and combine with bread crumbs, parsley, salt, pepper and rosemary. Stir in with melted butter and mix. Then trim fat off chops. Cut a pocket in each and pack crumb mixture inside pockets. Close with toothpicks if necessary.

Now. In a skillet heat 3 tbsp. oil until hot. Add chops and sauté about 4 min. on each side. Then remove chops and pour off fat from pan. To the pan add ½ c. chicken broth and ¼ c. white wine, stirring and scraping bottom of pan. Return the now chubby chops to the pan and bake at 350° for 20 min. Serve.

*baked stuffed

34.

LiveR foR the 1 out of 4 Americans ~~~ who won't eat it ~~~

6 (👌👌) slices calves liver
salt and pepper
flouR
Milk
4 tbsp. ButteR
2 tbsp. oil
½ c Beef Bouillon
1 tbsp. soft ButteR
few dRops Lemon juice
2 tbsp. fResh chopped paRsLey

MaRinate LiveR In milk foR 2-3 HOURS. That tames it. And Makes suRe it's dead. Remove, season with salt and peppeR and dip LightLy in flouR. In Heavy 12" skillet, melt butteR and oil oveR HigH Heat. When the foam disappears, sauté LiveR foR 2-3 min. on each side. Then Remove LiveR and keep it waRm. PouR off fat from skillet, add Bouillon and cook oveR HigH Heat stiRRing constantly till it gets syRupy and Reduced to ¼ cup. Then Remove pan from heat and mix in 1 tbsp. ButteR and a few dRops of Lemon juice. PouR oveR LiveR and spRinkLe with paRsLey.

35.

if
you
ain't
WHERE
you
aRe
you're
nowHere.

wanda
wallenda

some nice veal

1 LB. veal	3 tsp. flour
2 tBsp. Butter	½ c. white wine
2 tBsp. olive oil	2 c. sliced fresh
2 onions cut in	MUSHROOMS
SLIVERS	⅔ c. Half and Half

minced fresh parsley

Cut veal into thin strips and dredge lightly in flour. Brown veal strips and onions in butter and olive oil. Remove meat and onions and sprinkle flour in pan. Blend in white wine. Return meat and onions to skillet and add mushrooms stirring and cooking for about 2-3 minutes then blend in half and half. Reheat without boiling and sprinkle with parsley. Serve with buttered noodles or rice. There. you have some nice veal.

CHINESE PEPPER STEAK

2 LBS. Round Steak
2 Chicken Bouillon cubes
2 tbsp. Cornstarch
2 med. tomatoes sliced
2 Green peppers cut in strips

1 c. water
¾ c. water
2 oz. soy sauce
1 tsp. sugar
Garlic juice
2 tbsp. peanut oil

Mix cornstarch with ¾ c. water in a bowl and set aside. Bring 1 c. water to a boil in saucepan. Add soy sauce, mashed bouillon cubes, cornstarch mixture, few drops of garlic juice and sugar. Heat till thick. Cut round steak into strips and fry in peanut oil. Cool and drop into sauce. Add tomatoes and peppers. Heat 1 minute and serve with rice.

A Pretty Funny Joke

Tee Hee Hee. Did you hear that Hickory Farms is opening a new store in Jerusalem? They're calling it "Cheeses of Nazareth."

WHA-HA-H-A-HAH.

ARRIBA ARRIBA CASSEROLE

1 LB. GROUND BEEF
½ c. CHOPPED ONION
1 clove GARLIC minced
1 15-oz. can tomato sauce
12 soft corn tortillas
1 PKG. taco seasoning Mix

½ tsp. salt
¼ tsp. pepper
½ c. WATER
4 oz CREAM CHEESE
1 c. SHREDDED CHEDDAR

Blend taco seasoning Mix with ⅓ cup water, bring to a boil and simmer, that's 5 minutes. In a skillet cook GROUND BEEF, onion, GARLIC, salt and pepper till meat is BROWNED. DRain. Combine taco mix with tomato sauce. Stir together 1 c. of sauce mix with meat and set aside. Then spread one side of each tortilla with cream cheese. Put about ¼ c. meat mixture in the center of each tortilla and fold in Half. Place these open side up in a baking dish. Combine Remaining tomato-taco sauce mixture with ½ c. water. Pour over tortillas. Sprinkle cheddar on top. Bake covered at 375° for 25 min. Bake uncovered 5 min. more. Bueno. Bueno. Bueno.

CLEOPATRA'S CHILI

(the most coveted dish on the banks of the nile)

1 c. dried pinto beans
5 c. canned tomatoes
1 lb. green pepper
1½ tbsp. salad oil
1½ lbs. chopped onion
2 garlic cloves crushed
2½ lbs. ground chuck
1 lb. ground lean pork

½ c. chopped parsley
½ c. butter
⅓ c. chili powder
2 tbsp. salt
1½ tsp. pepper
1½ tsp. cumin seed

Wash pinto beans and soak overnight in water 2" above the beans. Next morning or whenever simmer the cute little pintos in the same water till all water is absorbed. Add tomatoes and simmer 5 min. more. In another pan sauté green pepper and onion in salad oil for about 5 min. Add garlic and parsley. Melt butter and cook meats. Then combine onion, meats and everything together and cook 1 hour. Uncover and cook 30 min. more. Skim fat off top. Serve with crackers and shredded cheddar. Julius Caesar died for this.

LOW-CALORIE CASSEROLE*

1½ LBS. GROUND CHUCK   1 tsp. salt

¾ c. CHOpped onion   ⅛ tsp. pepper

2 8-oz cans tomato sauce   8 oz. cream cheese

1 c. cottage cheese   ¼ c. sour cream

⅓ c. Green pepper CHOpped   ½ c. Green onion CHOpped

8 oz. Noodles cooked, cooled, drained

Brown meat and onion. Add salt, pepper and tomato sauce. Simmer slowly. Combine cottage cheese, cream cheese, sour cream, green pepper and green onion. Place ½ of noodles in a 3 qt. casserole. Top with cheese mixture. Then rest of noodles. Pour meat mixture over it all. Bake at 350° for 30 min. Serves 8-10.

Fat. Fat. Fat.

* That's a lie.

41.

Baked Stuffed Peppers
(that you don't have to bake)

↑ those are not pumpkins

3 medium Green peppers
1 tsp. sugar
½ tsp. Basil
1 15-oz. can tomato sauce
1 Lb. Ground Beef
1 small chopped onion
2 ¼ c. minute Rice
1 tsp. salt
2 c. water
2 tsp. Butter
½ c. Grated cheddar

Cut peppers in half this way ⬦. Boil in salted water for 10 min. then drain. Add sugar and Basil to tomato sauce then set aside. Brown Ground Beef and onion. Stir in ½ c. tomato mixture, ¼ c. uncooked Rice and ½ tsp. salt. Cover and simmer for 5 min. Stir in cheese. Spoon mixture into peppers and put in a skillet. Pour Remaining sauce around peppers, cover and simmer 5 min. Meanwhile, Bring water, ½ tsp. salt and Butter to Boil, stir in Rest of Rice, cover and let stand. Serve peppers over Rice. TAH-DAH.

TACO SALAD

4 medium tomatoes
1 medium looking onion
1½ lb. ground beef
8 oz. grated cheddar
tabasco sauce
1 15-oz. can kidney beans
1 head lettuce
1 8-oz. bottle thousand-island,
   catalina or red russian dressing
1 bag taco chips
12 taco shells

Brown hamburger and add kidney beans.
Simmer for 10 min. Dice tomatoes, onion,
lettuce. Mix in big bowl. Add grated
cheese. Add bottle of dressing and mix.
Crush taco chips and mix in. Add hamburger
and bean mixture. Add tabasco, salt and
pepper to taste. Mix all together.
Scoop into taco shells. Serve quickly
after mixing. Makes a lot.

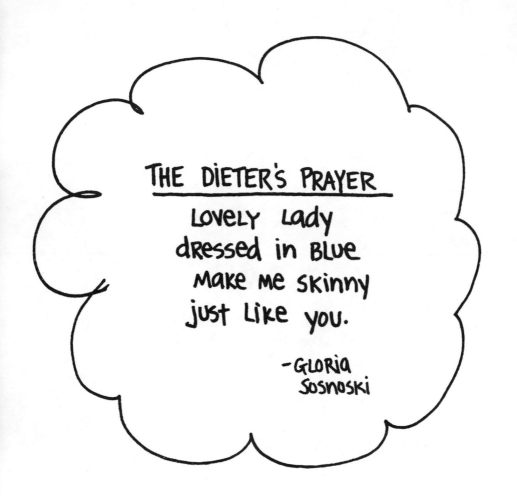

THE DIETER'S PRAYER

Lovely lady
dressed in blue
make me skinny
just like you.

–Gloria
Sosnoski

44.

JUMBO SHELLS
STUFFED WITH RICOTTA CHEESE

18 JUMBO SHeLLs
3 c. Ricotta cheese stuffing (see ☺☺ Recipe)
4 c. meat and tomato sauce (see ☺☺ Recipe)
2 tBsp. parmesan cheese

1. PReHeat oven to 400°
2. DRop JUMBOS into BoiLing water and cook about 10 min. DRain.
3. Spoon Layer of sauce over Bottom of casseRole LaRge enough to hold stuffed shells in one Layer.
4. Fill each SHell with cheese mixture. ARRange shells stuffed side up. Spoon Remaining sauce all over. Sprinkle with parmesan cheese. Bake 25 min. Six servings.

RICOTTA CHEESE

1 LB. Ricotta
½ c. diced mozzarella
pinch nutmeg
¼ c. prosciutto chopped fine

1 egg slightly Beaten
2 tBsp. chopped parsley
¼ c. parmesan

Combine in mixing Bowl. Use to stuff JUMBOs.

MEAT AND TOMATO SAUCE

4 c. imported canned tomatoes

¼ c. olive oil

1 tsp. garlic minced fine

½ c. onion chopped fine

½ lb. ground chuck

salt to taste

¼ c. tomato paste

¼ c. parsley chopped fine

2 tbsp. fresh basil chopped or ½ amount dried

½ tsp. dried hot pepper flakes

1. Cook tomatoes in saucepan 30 min. or until reduced to 3 cups.

2. Heat oil and add garlic and onion. Cook and stir until it all wilts. Add meat and cook about one minute.

3. Add tomatoes, salt, pepper and tomato paste. Stir to blend. Add parsley, basil and pepper flakes. Cook, stir 10 min. Makes 4 cups.

FACT

Many men but very few women have been impostors.

Fettucine Alfredo Primavera

that's 2 pints Half and Half
1 stick sweet cream butter
1/4 c. grated parmesan cheese
1/4 c. grated romano cheese
1/2 lb. spinach noodles (green)
1/2 lb. white egg noodles

1 bunch broccoli
5 carrots sliced thin→
freshly ground pepper
1/2 lb. fresh mushrooms sliced

Melt butter in skillet. Pour in half and half. While that's going on steam broccoli (the flower parts)+carrots till tender. Cook noodles as directed on package. Add parmesan and romano cheese to cream mixture. Sprinkle freshly ground pepper. Add now tender vegetables to sauce stirring slowly. Add mushrooms. Put noodles (both kinds) in a big bowl. Pour sauce over and mix well. Sprinkle with fresh ground pepper and parmesan.

CUTE LEG OF LAMB

1 LEG OF LAMB
1 CLOVE OF GARLIC
1 C. MEDIUM-SWEET RED WINE
½ C. WATER
1 tsp. OREGANO
SALT AND PEPPER

MAKE LITTLE CUTS ALL OVER THE
MEAT AND INSERT BITS OF GARLIC.
MIX WATER AND WINE AND POUR OVER
LAMB. YOU CAN USE MORE WINE IF
YOU LIKE. SEASON WITH SALT AND
PEPPER AND OREGANO. ROAST at 325°
FOR 30 MIN. PER POUND. COVER WITH
FOIL. MAKES IT COOK FASTER. BASTE
FREQUENTLY. POOR LAMB. LUCKY YOU.

THE
STORY OF
PRINDERELLA
AND THE
CINCE

→

Twonce upon a wine there was a Gritty little perl named Prinderella who lived with her micked wepstother and her two sisty uglers. Now the micked wepstother and her two sisty uglers made poor prinderella wean the clindows, flub the scoors and do all the wirty dirk. Now there was going to be this drancy fess ball and prinderella couldn't go because all she had to wear was her wirty dag. So she crat down and scried when all of a sudden her merry fodmother appeared and changed her wirty dag into a drancy fess and her crumpkin into a parraige and said "Off you go to the drancy fess ball to prance all night with the Cince, but you must be home by the moke of stridnight." So off she went to the drancy fess ball where she pranced all night

with the cince. Now while Prinderella
was joyously prancing with the
cince, she heard the clock strike
and at the moke of stridnight
she stashed down the stalace
paircase and what do you think
happened? Well i'll tell you. On
the stottom bep she slopped her
dripper. Wasn't that a shirty dame?
The cince missed his painty dartner
at the dance and looked ligh and ho
for her but couldn't find her
anywhere.

So the ping issued a croclamation
that all of the gelligible erls in the
pingdom should try on Prinderella's
dainty slass glipper. But their
fig beet just fidn't dit. But
Prinderella's finy toot fid dit so
they married and lived lappily
after everwards.

the end.

ALI YELLA'S BAKED FISH ORIENTALE

4-6 LB. WHOLE STRIPED BASS, TROUT, RED SNAPPER
(OR CUT PIECES)

SPRINKLE with olive oil, salt and red paprika.
CHOP up one BUNCH of PARSLEY and SPRINKLE
all over fish.

4 BUNCHES of scallions cut up and SPRINKLED
all over.

1 C SHERRY. POUR all over.

4-5 cloves GARLIC tossed HERE and there.

2 16-oz. cans tomatoes (OR fresh ones). POUR
over all.

1 C water. POUR over.

1 tsp. wine VINEGAR SPRINKLED over all.

Put fish in BAKING pan and POUR
ingredients all over. COVER pan with
foil and BAKE at 350° FOR 1 HOUR.
Take foil off Last 15 minutes. That
Gives it a Roasted flavor.

THIS ORIGINATES from a CHARMING
family on CHARLES street in Greenwich
village.

another nice fish dish

2 6-oz. white fish fillets (kind of firm)
salt both sides and dip in 1 slightly
beaten egg white.

Then roll in a mixture of:

> ⅓ c. seasoned bread crumbs
> ½ tsp. seasoned salt
> ¼ tsp. white pepper

Sauté 5 min. each side in:

> 1 tbsp. olive oil
> 1 tbsp. butter

While those babies are cooking make
this sauce: In a skillet melt 1 tbsp.
butter. Add 1 tbsp. flour and stir.
Then blend in ½ c. milk, 2 tbsp. fresh
lemon juice, ¼ tsp. salt. Cook over
medium heat till it starts to thicken.
Cook and stir (without boiling) until
sauce gets real thick. Then stir in
3 tbsp. minced parsley. Pour sauce
over fish and serve. Can also add
cheese, basil and almonds if you
like.

SHRIMP CREOLE

1½ LBS. RAW SHRIMP
4 tBsp. Butter
1 c. CHopped onion
2 small celery sticks
    CHopped
3 cloves Garlic minced
2 c. canned italian
    tomatoes
1 Green pepper
    Chopped

½ tsp. thyme
1 Bay Leaf
tabasco to taste
Salt + pepper to taste
3 tBsp. parsley
juice of ½ Lemon

SHELL SHRIMP. Rinse. Pat dry. Melt Butter
in Large pan and add onion. Cook on
medium Heat till onion is weak and wilted.
Add celery, Green pepper and Garlic.
Cook for a short time making sure
veggies stay crisp. Add tomatoes, thyme,
Bay Leaf, tabasco, Lemon juice, salt and
pepper. Simmer 10 min. Don't cover.
Add the shrimp, cover and cook no
Longer than 3-5 min. Add parsley
and if some Like it Hot more tabasco.
Serve as is with crackers or over
Rice. Serves 2-4.

SHRIMP BOILED IN BEER
(WHAT A WAY TO GO)

1 LB. RAW SHRIMP (LEAVE SHELLS ON)
1 BAY LEAF
ABOUT 15 PEPPERCORNS
1 FRESH LEMON SLICE
dashes of TABASCO
5 whole allspice
1 CAN BEER
salt to taste

Put all of that in a BIG pan and add enough water to cover the shrimp. BRING it all to a boil...then let the SHRIMP cool in that LIQUID. serve with cocktail sauce on p. 21. Makes enough for 4.

★ Ain't it the truth ★

the things most people want to know are usually none of their business.

MEMBERS OF THE * SUPPORTING CAST

CLAP CLAP " " "WAHOO" " BREAK A LEG

"WOOPTY DOO"

HURRAY

ALL RIGHT!

SHAKE IT ON OUT " "YIPEE"

ON WITH THE SHOW

* SIDE DISHES

56.

How to make very perfect rice

    2 c. raw long grain rice
    3 c. water

Rinse rice in pan 3-4 times to remove starch. Add 3c. water to rice and bring to a rapid boil. Cook uncovered over high heat till water disappears and little steam vents can be seen on the surface of the rice. Then cover tightly and continue cooking over very low heat for 12 min. Fluff rice before serving. Makes 5-6 cups.

"There are moments when this city can jolt us with the certainty that we'd rather be alive right here and now than anywhere else on earth at any time whatever."
    <u>the new yorker</u>   july 1981   57.

PRETTY SNAPPY RICE

1 c. uncooked Rice
2 c. Chicken Broth
1/4 c. Red Bell pepper chopped
1/4 c. Green pepper chopped
1/4 c. Green onion chopped
2 tBsp. Butter
salt
dash of tabasco

Cook Rice accordingly, using chicken Broth instead of water. Sauté peppers and onions in Butter for 2-3 min. Stir into cooked Rice. Season to taste. Serves four with zip and snap.

STRANGE BUT TRUE

Shirley temple looked just like KAROL jackowski when she was little.

58.

a nice potato casserole

6 medium-looking potatoes
1 pt. sour cream
10 oz. cheddar cheese grated
Bunch of green onions, diced
3 tbsp. milk
1 tsp. salt
pepper to taste
combine: 2 tbsp. melted butter
          1/3 c. bread crumbs

Cook potatoes. Cool potatoes.
Peel and grate potatoes. Add
remaining ingredients. Turn
into a 9 x 13 pan. Top with
buttered bread crumbs.
Bake at 300° for 50 min.

one potato. two potato. three potato. four. five potato.

MAGIC VEGETABLE BAKE

¼ c. margarine
½ c. cornflakes crushed
¼ c. parmesan cheese
1 c. french style green beans
1 c. cooked cauliflower
1 c. sliced cooked carrots
2 tsp. onions
1 c. grated cheddar
1 can. mushroom soup
1 c. sliced cooked potatoes

Melt margarine. Add crumbs and parmesan cheese. Set aside for topping. Place everything else in a casserole. Mix. Sprinkle with topping. Bake 30-45 min. at 350°. Pretty tasty.

THREE  BEAN BAKE

1 16-oz. can Lima Beans, drained
1 16-oz. can navy Beans, drained
1 16-oz. can Kidney Beans, drained
3 tbsp. oil
2 medium onions chopped
3/4 c. catsup
3 tbsp. vinegar
2 Tbsp. Brown sugar
2 tsp. salt
1 Tbsp. mustard
1 c. Bar-B-Que potato chips, crushed

Sauté onions in oil until light Brown.
Add Brown sugar, vinegar, catsup,
salt, mustard and mix well. Add
Beans and mix. Pour into 2 qt.
casserole and top with crushed
chips. Bake at 325° for 1 HR.
Wonderful if you like a lot of
Beans. Absolutely wonderful.

cute acorn squash

2 acorn squash (cute ones)
½ c. Hot water
4 tbsp. melted butter
4 tbsp. Brown sugar
nut meg

Cut the cute squashes in Half and take the seeds out. Place cut side down in a shallow baking pan. Add the Hot water which will keep the cute Little things moist. Bake at 350° for 45 min. Then turn over and inside the spot where the seeds were, in each Half, put:

1 tbsp. butter
1 tbsp. Brown sugar
sprinkle of nutmeg

Bake 15 min. more. Baste one or two times. Serve.

★ AUNTIE LILLY'S GREEN BEANS ★

¼ c. BUTTER

1 c. BREAD CRUMBS

1 LARGE can GREEN BEANS OR
    parts equivalent of fresh ones
(love to say "parts equivalent")

If using fresh beans... steam till tender. If using canned beans open the can and drain.

Melt butter in a skillet and add bread crumbs. Stir around and mix well. Add beans and stir around some more covering beans with crumbs and getting them hot. When they look nice and taste good and hot... serve.

A WORD FROM MAE WEST

I used to be Snow White, but
        I drifted.

63.

SWEET AND SOUR CABBAGE FROM MONTANA

1 head of cabbage
6 slices of bacon
2 tsp. chopped onion
½ c. brown sugar (round, firm and
                    fully packed)
1 tsp. cornstarch
1 tsp. salt
¼ c. cold water
⅓ c. vinegar

Chop cabbage and boil till tender. (Boil till tender... boil till sweet... never let it go). Cook bacon till crisp. Drain and crumble. Reserve 3 tbsp. of drippings in skillet. To the drippings add 2 tsp. chopped onion, brown sugar, cornstarch, salt, water and vinegar. Cook and stir constantly until thick and clear. Add bacon. Drain cabbage. Pour mixture over cabbage and serve. Let mixture cool a little before you pour.

♀♀♀ teenie weenie creamed onions ♀♀♀

2 LBS. teenie weenie boiling onions
2 tbsp. Butter
2 tbsp. flour
1/4 tsp. salt
1 tsp. Basil
1/8 tsp. white pepper
1 c. light cream
2 tbsp. vermouth

Pour some boiling water over teenie weenie onions. Let them stand a few minutes then drain and peel. Drop peeled onions into some boiling salted water just enough to cover. Cook uncovered for about 15 min. Drain and put them aside for awhile. Then melt the butter and blend in the flour and seasonings. Stir till it ⟶BUBBLES. Add cream and vermouth. Cook and stir until the mixture thickens and boils 1 min. Add the teenie weenie's to sauce mix and serve 6 people.

NOT YOUR USUAL GREEN BEAN CASSEROLE

2 LBS. GREEN BEANS
1 5-oz. can water chestnuts
1 LB. Sliced Mushrooms
1 onion chopped
½ c. Butter
¼ c. flour
2 c. Milk
1 tsp. Parsley

¾ LB. Grated Cheddar Cheese
1 c. light cream
2 tsp. soy sauce
½ tsp. salt
½ tsp. Pepper
1 tsp. Basil
½ c. almonds

Wash Beans and Break in Half. Steam till tender. Drain and slice water chestnuts. Melt Butter. Sauté onion and Mushrooms. Stir in flour and cook 1-2 min. Slowly Blend in milk and cream. Cook and Stir till Mixture thickens and Boils. Add cheese, soy sauce, parsley, Basil, salt and pepper. Mix. Add Beans and chestnuts to sauce and stir. Put into Buttered casserole. Sprinkle almonds on top. Bake at 375° for 20 min. serves 6-8.

SOMEWHERE OVER THE RAINBOW

CAULIFLOWER

1 LARGE CAULIFLOWER
7 tBsp. BUTTER
1 CLOVE GARLIC
4 tBsp. CHOPPED ONION
2 tBsp. CHOPPED FRESH parsley
3 tBsp. BREAD CRUMBS

Cut and make nice Little Bunches of caulifowerettes. Steam until tender. Keep warm. Melt 4 tBsp. Butter in pan. Add onions and cook over low Heat a few minutes. Press Garlic and add to onion mixture. Cook till onions Get soft and wilt. Add parsley, crumbs and Rest of Butter. Mix with Cauliflower and serve.

YOUR STANDARD GLAZED CARROTS

12 carrots
salt
¼ LB. Butter
½ c white sugar
½ c. Brown sugar
½ c. carrot water
nutmeg

Peel carrots and cut in Half. Put in a pan, Barely cover with water and toss in a little salt. Boil for aBout 3 min. Drain But save ½ c. of the carrot water. Then melt Butter in skillet and add carrots, sugar and carrot water. sprinkle with a little nutmeg. cook till the Liquid disappears and the sugar Has dramatically and nicely Glazed and Browned carrots. ta-dah.

SHEEP DID NOT COME TO THE

68.

POTATO PANCAKES FOR  (THAT'S SIX)

6 POTATOES
2 EGGS
1 ½ tbsp. FLOUR
¼ tsp. BAKING POWDER
1 ¼ tsp. SALT
1 ONION GRATED
½ tsp. BASIL
½ tsp. PARSLEY
1 LB. LARD

GRATE POTATOES INTO LARGE MIXING BOWL.
BEAT EGGS AND ADD TO POTATOES. ADD
REST OF STUFF TO POTATO MIXTURE AND
MIX WELL. NEEDLESS TO SAY YOU DON'T
ADD THE LARD TO THE POTATO MIXTURE.
GROSS. YOU MELT THE LARD IN A SKILLET
ENOUGH TO MAKE ½". WHEN IT GETS REAL
HOT DROP IN THE POTATO BATTER BY THE
SPOONFUL MAKING NICE PATTIES. COOK TILL
CRISP ON BOTH SIDES.

UNITED STATES UNTIL 1609.

SWISS BEANS

1½ LBS. GReen Beans
2 tBsp. Butter
2 tBsp. flour
1 tsp. sugar
¼ tsp. pepper

½ tsp. Grated onion
1 C. sour cream
2 C. corn flakes
½ LB. Grated swiss cheese
2 tBsp. melted Butter

Wash the Beans and BReak in Half. Steam till tender and drain. Melt Butter in saucepan and stir in flour, sugar, pepper and onion. Cook a few minutes. Stir in the sour cream until it Gets smooth. Fold in the Beans. When all is well and folded put that In a ButteRed casserole dish. Sprinkle with cheese. CRush the corn flakes and Mix with the melted Butter. Scatter the flakes over the cheese. Bake at 375° for 30 min. Serves 6. YODLE-LEE-ODLE-LEE-ODLE-WHOOO...

70.

BROCCOLI IN A GENTLE WINE SAUCE

1½ LBS. BROCCOLI
1 CHICKEN BOUILLON CUBE
¾ c. BOILING water
¼ c. BUTTER
¼ c. flour
1 c. CREAM
1 tsp. BASIL

2 tbsp. SHERRY
2 tBsp. Lemon juice
½ tsp. MSG*
PEPPER
¼ c. parmesan cheese
¼ c. toasted almonds

Cut, trim and steam BROCCOLI about 5 min. Arrange cleverly in a baking dish. Melt butter, add flour and stir until it starts to BUBBLE. Melt the Bouillon ☐ in the Boiling water and Blend that with the cream into the flour mixture. Over medium Heat cook and stir constantly until it starts to Get thick and comes to a Boil. Add the sherry, lemon juice, MSG, basil and pepper (to taste). Pour over the cleverly arranged BROCCOLI. Sprinkle with parmesan and almonds. Bake at 375° for 20 min.

*MONOSODIUM GLUTAMATE NOT MADISON
   SQUARE GARDEN

LITTLE CABBAGES IN CHEESE SAUCE

1½ LBS. BRUSSELS SPROUTS
8 OZ. SHREDDED CHEDDAR CHEESE
¼ C. SOUR CREAM
2 tBSP. LIGHT CREAM
1 tSP. BASIL
1 tSP. LEMON JUICE
½ tSP. WORCESTERSHIRE SAUCE
¼ tSP. SALT
¼ C. SLIVERED ALMONDS

Blend cheddar cheese, sour cream and light cream in top of double boiler. Stir until well blended then add basil, lemon juice, w. sauce and salt. It should look like pouring consistency. If it's not add more cream. Keep this sauce warm. Cook brussels sprouts in boiling water about 8 min. Drain and put them in a serving dish. Pour hot sauce over them and sprinkle almonds on top.

"OW" GRATIN POTATOES

8 tbsp. Butter
6 potatoes
salt and pepper
1 tsp. Basil
3 tsp. flour
8 oz. Grated cheddar cheese
2 c. scalded milk

Smear 2 tbsp. Butter over the Bottom of casserole dish. Peel and slice potatoes. Put them in a pot and add enough water to cover. Boil 5 min. Drain well. Place a layer of potatoes in dish. Sprinkle with salt, pepper and 1 tsp. flour. Dot . . . . . with 2 tbsp. Butter and cover with ½ c. cheese. Repeat the layers twice more and end up with cheese on top. Pour milk over it all and Bake at 350° for 40 min.

✿ ✿ ✿ BROCCOLI A LA ✿ ✿ ✿
JUST ABOUT EVERYTHING

2 LBS. BROCCOLI
1 stick Butter melted
Parmesan cheese
3 tbsp. Butter
3 tbsp. flour
salt, cayenne pepper, celery salt
1 c. milk
1 tbsp. Lemon juice
3 tbsp. orange juice
heavy cream
Blanched slivered almonds

Wash off the Broccoli and trim off the stems so you just have the cute little flowerettes ❧ *those are not hands.* Steam Broccoli about 5 min. then drain and Rinse in cold water. Melt 1 stick Butter and dip those little flowerettes in it. Place nicely in a casserole dish and sprinkle well with Parmesan cheese. Then melt 3 tbsp. Butter and stir in flour, ½ tsp. salt, sprinkles of cayenne and

½ tsp. celery salt. Cook about 1-2 min. Then blend in 1 c milk over low heat. Stir until it starts to get thick and boils. Add lemon and orange juice and more cream if needed to thin out sauce and make it smooth like flannel and creamy. Spread it nicely over broccoli. Bake at 425° for 15 min. or until sauce bubbles and almonds are brown. A tasty little number.

★ A FASCINATING FACT ★

A SICK PIG RARELY CURLS HIS TAIL.

QUIZ: WHICH PIG IS SICK?
(CLUE: THE ABOVE OBJECTS ARE PIGS)

RILED WILD RICE

⅓ c. oil
½ c. chopped celery
¼ c. chopped parsley
½ c. minced green onion
1½ c. wild rice
1 10-oz. can chicken stock
1½ c. boiling water

1 tsp. salt
½ tsp. basil
½ tsp. marjoram
½ c. white wine

Heat oil in skillet. Add parsley, onion and celery. Cook till tender. Wash rice real well. Add to skillet with chicken stock, water, salt, basil and marjoram. Cover and cook over low heat 45 min. Stir rice every few minutes. If it becomes too dry add a little more boiling water. When rice is tender and water absorbed stir in white wine. Leave uncovered and cook 3-5 min. longer. Serve wild and now riled rice to 6.

that's 𝄞🤙.

ENCORE
ENCORE

WE WANT MORE

CLAP
CLAP
CLAP
CLAP
CLAP

AUTHOR!
AUTHOR!

COME ON...
ON WITH THE SHOW.

DYNAMITE.

MORE. MORE. MORE.

WOWEE.

DESSERTS
GIVE US
DESSERTS!!!

YOUR JUST DESSERTS

(the kind you would like to get...)

↑
AN OBVIOUSLY DELIGHTED
CREATURE OF GOD
DEMONSTRATING WHAT ONE
MIGHT LOOK LIKE AFTER HAVING
HAD THEIR JUST DESSERTS.

CARAMEL – FILLED BROWNIES

1 BAG Kraft caramels (Light ones)
2/3 c. evaporated milk
1 German chocolate cake mix
1/3 c. melted butter
1 c. chopped nuts
1 c. chocolate chips

Combine 1/3 c. evaporated milk and caramels and melt in a double Boiler. Combine melted butter, 1/3 c. evaporated milk, cake mix and nuts. Mix well and press 1/2 mixture into greased 9 x 13 pan. Bake that at 350° for 6 min. Remove from oven and sprinkle chocolate chips on top....then spread caramel mix on top then remaining cake mixture. Bake at 350° for 15-18 min.

*SHORTBREADS

1 LB. BUTTER
1⅓ c. powdered sugar
½ tsp. salt
4 c. flour
1½ tsp. vanilla

Cream butter and sugar.
Add salt, flour and vanilla. Mix.
Make into whatever shapes
(little squares are nice) and
press onto greased cookie
sheet. Bake at 325° about
12 min. Very very rich and
very very good.

* MAMMY'S LITTLE BABY LOVES
THESE.

MONSTER

6 eggs
1 LB. BROWN SUGAR
1½ tBsp. vanilla
1½ tBsp. white corn
                syrup
½ LB. Butter
1½ LB. peanut Butter
4 tsp. Baking soda

9 c. oatmeal
½ LB. chocolate
            chips
½ LB. M+M's

Mix ingredients in order given.
Drop on cookie sheet By large
tablespoons... flatten slightly.
Bake 12 min. at 350°.
Do not overbake. Makes 8½ doz.
These are rather incredible.

COOKIES

ORANGE - PINEAPPLE JELLO

2 3-oz. pks. orange jello
1 3-oz. tapioca pudding mix
2 c. boiling water
1 lrg. can crushed pineapple
1 lrg. can mandarin oranges
1 8-oz. container Cool Whip

Dissolve jello and tapioca with the 2 c. boiling water. Put in freezer till it starts to slush. Add drained pineapple and oranges. Put back into freezer until it starts to slush again. Then mix in Cool Whip.

This makes a lot. Use a very large mold or put into shallow pan and cut into squares. After adding Cool Whip keep in fridge. This is nice.

BOHEMIAN CRESCENTS

1 c. butter
½ c. confectioners sugar
1 tsp. vanilla
2 c. sifted cake flour
1 c. chopped nuts

Cream butter and blend in sugar; then add vanilla. Add flour gradually, stirring after each addition until smooth. Stir in chopped nuts. Dip fingers into dough and shape into crescents. Place on ungreased cookie sheet and bake at 350° for 15-20 min. When cool sprinkle with confectioners sugar.

HO-HO CAKE

NOTE: YES. THIS IS HO-HO AS IN DING-DONGS, ZINGERS AND KOO-KOO'S AND DEVIL DOGS AND LITTLE DEBBIES.

First make 1 chocolate fudge cake mix per instructions on the box and spread in a large greased pan, 12 × 18 × ¾. Bake at 350° for about 15 min. Cool.

FILLING: Cook 5 tbsp. flour and 1½ c. milk until thick. Let cool. Then put that in a mixing bowl with 1 stick margarine, ½ c. shortening and 1 c. sugar. Beat on HIGH speed until light and fluffy (about 8-10 min). Then spread this nice white fluff evenly over the top of cake to about ¼" from the edge of the pan. CHILL.

-MORE-

HO-HO FROSTING

Melt 1 stick margarine and cool slightly. Add 1 egg, 3 squares semi-sweet chocolate melted, 1 tsp. vanilla, 2½ tbsp. hot water and 1½ c. powdered sugar. Beat smooth by hand. Spread immediately over cake, clear to the edge of the pan. Keep in fridge until served. Cut into squares.

This is a must for those, who like me, invest weekly in Ho-Ho's, Ding Dongs, Zingers, Koo-Koo's, Devil Dogs or Little Debbies. It could change your life.

THOSE ARE
PECANS ↙

PECAN PIE

Pastry for 9" pie shell
1 c. pecan halves
3 eggs
1 tbsp. melted butter
1 c. light corn syrup
½ tsp. vanilla
1 c. sugar
1 tbsp. flour

Arrange pecans in bottom of unbaked pie shell. Beat eggs. Add butter and corn syrup and vanilla. Stir until well blended. Combine sugar, flour and blend in egg mixture. Pour over nuts in pie shell. Let stand until the nuts magically rise to the surface. Bake at 350° for 45 min. Nuts glaze all by themselves during baking.

"THERE'S no use trying" SHE said,
"one can't believe impossible
   things."

"I daresay you Haven't Had
   MUCH practice," said the Queen.
"WHEN I was your age I always
   did it for Half-an-Hour a day.
   WHY, sometimes I believed as
   many as six impossible things
   before breakfast."

Alice
   in
WonderLand

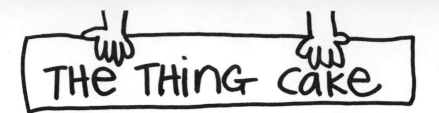

THE THING CAKE

Preheat oven to 350°. Grease well a 9x13 pan. Then take:

- 1 pkg. yellow cake mix
- 1 stick butter
- 1 c. chopped pecans
- 1 egg

Mix together. Mixture will be real thick. Spread mixture into pan.

Next take:

- 8oz. cream cheese
- 1 box (1 lb) powdered sugar
- 2 eggs

Mix that well and pour over thick mixture. Bake 45 min. Serve warm or cold.

There was a star danced and under that i was born.

W. Shakespeare

TAPPITY TAP

TAP TAP

CARROT  CAKE

2 c. flour
2 tsp. Baking powder
1 tsp. salt
1½ tsp. Baking soda
2 tsp. cinnamon
2 c. sugar

1½ c. oil
4 eggs
2 c. grated carrots
1 8½-oz. can crushed pineapple
½ c. chopped nuts

Combine flour, B. powder, salt, soda and cinnamon. Add sugar, oil and eggs. Mix well. Add carrots, pineapple (drained) and nuts. Bake in 9x13 greased and floured pan at 350° for 40 min.

FROSTING

½ c. Butter
8 oz. cream cheese
1 tsp. vanilla

1 lb. powdered sugar
Milk

Cream butter, cheese and vanilla. Add sugar. If too thick add milk to spreading consistency.

Serves 12.

CHOCOLATE ECLAIR WAZOO

2 PKS. instant french vanilla pudding
3¾ c. milk
Mix for 2-3 min.
Then fold in 8 oz. cool whip.
Then Line a 9×13 pan with whole graham crackers.
Then put ½ of the pudding mix on the graham crackers. Then another layer of graham crackers. Then rest of pudding mix. Then take a can of soft chocolate frosting and frost graham crackers individually and set on top of pudding mix. Chill and serve.

WAZOO

"WOW."

"WHAT A BOOK."

"CLAP CLAP"

"I'LL TAKE TEN."

"CLAP CLAP"

"AUTHOR! AUTHOR!"

"PULITZER! PULITZER!"

"MORE. MORE."

"MAKE A MOVIE!"

"OPEN A RESTAURANT!"

"WHAT A NUN!"

"TAKE THIS ACT ON THE ROAD!"

INDISPENSABLE INDEX

CAKES
- Carrot, 89
- Ho-Ho, 84
- the thing, 88

CARROTS
- Glazed, 68
- Vegetable Bake, 60

CAULIFLOWER
- Seasoned, 67

CHICKEN
- amazing jen-sen, 23
- Gizzards, 24
- hot chicken salad, 30
- "knock your socks off," 26
- Livers, 25
- "Rocky 4", 28

COOKIES
- Bohemian crescents, 83
- Caramel-filled brownies, 79
- Monster cookies, 81
- Short breads, 80

DESSERTS
- Chocolate eclair wazoo, 90
- Orange-pineapple jello, 82

DIPS

Guacamole, 12
Vegetable, 15

FISH AND SHELLFISH

Baked fish Orientale, 52
fish dish, 53
Shrimp Boiled in Beer, 55
Shrimp Creole, 54

FROSTINGS

Cream cheese, 89
Ho-Ho, 85

LAMB

Cute leg of lamb, 48

LIVER

Beef, 35
Chicken, 25

MACARONI MAIN DISHES

fettucine Alfredo primavera, 47
Low-calorie casserole, 41
Jumbo shells, 45

MARINADE

Beef and chicken, 31

ONIONS

Creamed, 65

PIE
pecan, 86

PORK
barbecued ribs, 33
stuffed pork chops, 34

POTATOES
au gratin, 73
casserole, 59
pancakes, 69
vegetable bake, 60

RICE
perfect, 57
snappy, 58
riled wild, 76

SALAD DRESSINGS
celery seed, 14
gin, 13
poppy seed, 13
vinaigrette, 11, 14

SALADS
artichoke, 10
cucumber, 9
fruit, 8
spinach, 7
taco, 43

SAUCES

    BROWN, 19
    CHEESE, 19
    COCKTAIL, 21
    HERB BUTTER, 20
    HERB SALT, 21
    LEMON BUTTER, 11
    MEAT AND TOMATO, 46
    VINAIGRETTE, 11, 14
    WHITE, 17
    WHITE WINE, 20

SHELLFISH

    SEE 88 FISH

SQUASH

    ACORN, 62

VEAL,

    WITH MUSHROOMS, 37

THE END